Quiz # 13098
B.L. 4.6
Pts. 0.5

AMAZING RAIN FOREST

RAIN FORESTS

Lynn Stone

The Rourke Corporation, Inc.
Vero Beach, Florida 32964

Printed in the U.S.A.

PHOTO CREDITS
All photos © Lynn M. Stone except title page and p. 12 © James
H. Carmichael and p. 21 © Breck P. Kent

Library of Congress Cataloging-in-Publication Data

Stone, Lynn M.
  The amazing rain forest / by Lynn M. Stone
     p. cm. — (Discovering the rain forest)
  Includes index
  ISBN 0-86593-392-8
  1. Rain forest ecology—Juvenile literature. 2. Rain forests—
Juvenile literature. [1. Rain forests.]
I. Title   II. series: Stone, Lynn M.   Discovering the rain forest
QH541.5.R27S75 1994
574.5'2642—dc20   94-20909
                                                            CIP
                                                            AC

TABLE OF CONTENTS

THE AMAZING TROPICAL RAIN FOREST

The tropical rain forests of the world are indeed amazing. They are amazingly green, wet and wild.

They are also amazingly rich in plant and animal life. Perhaps one-half of the **species**, or kinds, of plants and animals that live on Earth are found in the tropical rain forests. Yet tropical rain forests cover less than one-tenth of the world's land surface.

The world's great, green tropical rain forests hold an amazing variety of life

GROWING A TROPICAL RAIN FOREST

The world's tropical region, or "tropics," broadly follows the **equator**. The equator is an imaginary line around the middle of the Earth.

Many tropical forests receive heavy rainfall, more than 80 inches each year. That is about twice as much moisture as New York or Chicago receives yearly.

The tropical rain forests grow where the average monthly temperature is 75 degrees (Fahrenheit) or more. Frost is unknown.

After a rain, mist hangs over a break in the rain forest canopy

WHERE THE RAIN FORESTS GROW

The largest tropical rain forest is in northern and eastern South America. Brazil alone has about 30 percent of the world's tropical rain forest.

Other large tropical rain forests are in West Africa and Southeast Asia. Smaller, scattered tropical rain forests are also in Central America, southern Mexico, northeastern Australia and on some Caribbean and South Pacific islands.

Protected tropical rain forest clings to the hills and valleys of Braulio Carillo National Park, Costa Rica

THE RAIN FOREST CANOPY

All tropical rain forests look somewhat alike from a distance. They are jungles of ferns, vines, trees, bushes and other plants whose leaves stay green year around.

Each tropical rain forest grows in "layers." The top layer is the upper **canopy**, the "roof" of the forest. A few tall trees stand above the canopy. These trees with their mushroom-shaped crowns are the skyscrapers of the forest.

Looking down at a dense tropical rain forest canopy

Coatimundi prowls Central American rain forests at night

*This anole lizard, like many other rain forest creatures,
matches its surroundings*

THE UNDERSTORY AND BELOW

A dense, shrubby **understory** grows below the canopy. This layer of the forest is made up of palms, small trees and other plants.

The forest floor lies below the understory. Because so little sunlight reaches the floor, the plants are not thick. Without plenty of sunlight, green plants cannot grow well.

Although tropical rain forests look similar, each is different because of its **altitude** and general location.

Ferns and palm leaves in a rain forest understory bathe in a gentle rain

INSIDE THE TROPICAL RAIN FOREST

Most tropical rain forests have at least 200 rainy days each year. No wonder that tropical rain forests are often dripping wet. But some rain forests also have a dry period each year.

The air in a tropical rain forest is warm and **humid**, filled with moisture. The average temperature changes very little from one month to the next.

The forest floor and understory are dimly lit. Leaves and branches of the canopy block sunlight.

A butterfly lands in the shadows of a rain forest

PLANTS OF THE TROPICAL RAIN FOREST

The green rain forests are home to many kinds of animals because they are homes to many kinds of plants. Mosses, vines, flowers, trees and **epiphytes** are just a few of the plants that grow here.

Rain forest plants are well watered and well fed. Many of them grow throughout the year.

The roots of rain forest plants quickly take **nutrients**—healthy foods—from the soil. If they didn't work quickly, rains would carry these nutrients deep into the ground.

Epiphytes cover the branches of rain forest trees

ANIMALS OF THE RAIN FOREST

Scientists have identified thousands of species of plants and animals in the tropical rain forests. Thousands more await discovery.

Insects of all shapes and sizes live in tropical rain forests. Brightly colored birds live here, too, along with snakes and lizards, frogs and toads, and mammals.

Animals can be found from the litter of leaves on the rain forest floor to the crowns of tall trees.

White-handed tamarin is a rare monkey of South American rain forests

DISCOVERIES IN THE TROPICAL RAIN FORESTS

Long ago scientists found such well known products as cocoa and rubber in rain forests. More recently, scientists have been studying rain forest plants for possible use as medicines. Almost 100 species of tropical rain forest plants are already being used to make medicines.

Scientists will continue to find useful plants as they study these amazing forests and their **native** people.

Glossary

altitude (AL tuh tood) — the height of something above ground or sea level

canopy (KAN uh pee) — the "roof" of upper branches and leaves in a forest

epiphyte (EHP uh fite) — any of several kinds of plants that grow on other plants, usually trees, without harming the host plant

equator (ee KWAY ter) — the line drawn on maps around the earth's middle at equal distances from the north and south poles

humid (HU mid) — referring to moist, wet air

native (NAY tihv) — referring to people, plants or animals that are found naturally in an area, as being different from people, plants or animals that are brought into an area

nutrient (NU tree ent) — any of several "good" substances needed for health and growth

species (SPEE sheez) — a certain kind of plant or animal within a closely related group; for example a *poison-arrow* frog

understory (UN der stor ee) — the shrubby layer of small trees under the forest canopy

INDEX